Web

JOHN WYNDHAM

Level 5

Retold by Jocelyn Potter and Andy Hopkins
Series Editor: Derek Strange

Pearson Education Limited
Edinburgh Gate, Harlow,
Essex CM20 2JE, England
and Associated Companies throughout the world.

ISBN-13: 978-0-582-41697-0
ISBN-10: 0-582-41697-3

Designed by D W Design Partnership Ltd
Typeset by RefineCatch Limited, Bungay, Suffolk
Set in 11/14pt Monotype Bembo
Printed in China
SWTC/06

Published by Pearson Education Limited in association with
Penguin Books Ltd, both companies being subsidiaries of Pearson Plc

For a complete list of titles available in the Penguin Readers series please write to your local
Pearson Education office or contact: Penguin Readers Marketing Department,
Pearson Education, Edinburgh Gate, Harlow, Essex, CM20 2JE.

Contents

Introduction

David reached the tree and put his hand up to touch the white stuff that covered it. Then something seemed to fall on him, hiding him from us, and suddenly there was a loud scream.

The island of Tanakuatua in the Pacific Ocean is sunny and beautiful; the island of many people's dreams. And it is the place that the rich Lord Foxfield chooses for his dream – the creation of a new society, where everyone will live and work in peace.

But good dreams have a terrible way of turning bad. Something is wrong on Tanakuatua, very wrong . . .

John Wyndham (1903–69) was born in a village in Warwickshire, in the middle of England. His parents separated when he was eight years old, and after that he and his mother and brother constantly moved home, and Wyndham went to many different schools.

After leaving school he tried many jobs, including farming and advertising, before he turned to writing. He had little success until he began to write imaginative science stories like his hero, H. G. Wells. He sent these to American magazines and sold his first story to *Wonder Stories* in 1931. For the rest of the thirties, he enjoyed success in American and British magazines.

After World War II, he found that readers' tastes had changed. He spent some years unsuccessfully writing new stories until he wrote *The Day of the Triffids* (1951). This was very popular and Wyndham went on to write many more powerfully imaginative novels and stories. *Web* was the last novel he wrote and did not appear until ten years after his death.

Chapter 1   A New Society

'But how did you become involved in such a crazy business?'

That is the question I am always asked when the subject is mentioned, and it is the one I find most difficult to answer.

There is only one way I can explain it, even to myself. That is that I must have been suffering from delayed shock – a shock that upset my judgement. I *think* that may have been the cause.

Almost a year before I met Tirrie and so became 'involved in the crazy business', I had a nasty accident.

My daughter, Mary, was driving. I was beside her and my wife was in the back. We were going along the A272 towards Etchingham at about thirty-five miles an hour, when a lorry travelling at about fifty overtook us. I remember two sights quite clearly. The first was the wheels of the lorry sliding away from the side of our car; the second was the lorry falling towards us.

I woke up in a hospital bed a week later. Two more weeks passed before I was well enough to be told that my wife and Mary were both dead.

They let me out of hospital two months later. I felt empty and confused, and my life seemed to have little purpose. I left my job. I realize now that giving up work was the worst possible thing to do because it would perhaps have helped me to recover; at the time, though, work seemed so meaningless. I went to stay with my sister in Tonbridge, but continued to feel empty in both heart and mind.

That is the only way I can explain the enthusiasm I felt when I first heard of Lord Foxfield's Project. It felt as if I was waking from a long sleep, and I welcomed his dream of the future without thinking about any of the practical difficulties that it involved. But now it is gone, the dream destroyed.

◆

The original idea for the Project seems to have come at the same time to both Lord Foxfield and Walter Tirrie, and it grew in eager conversation between the two of them. Walter was an architect but was better known for his writings as a journalist; in these he often suggested bold solutions to social problems. Lord Foxfield had the necessary money and power, and Tirrie's friendship with him allowed him to develop these ideas into an actual plan.

But why was Lord Foxfield willing to support such a Project? The answer was simple. Like all rich men who have had power and position during their lives, he wanted people to remember him after his death, and he had spent more than two years searching for a special cause. He was an individualist who wished to be remembered for leading important social change, so he refused to become involved in anything that looked back to the past, and particularly avoided any Project which concerned animals.

It is quite certain that Walter Tirrie was not one of the many who approached him for money. It is likely that it was Foxfield who made contact with Tirrie after reading his angry words about social ills in the national press.

As the two men got to know each other better, and the plan developed, Lord Foxfield lost all interest in other people's ideas for his money; he had invented, or discovered, a special Project of his own.

The idea was very simple – although not original. Foxfield, however, had the power and the money to take it from the minds of dreamers and make it real. It was to build a free, politically independent society in which people were able to create a new way of life.

'The principles of the new society will be Knowledge and Reason,' said Lord F, to anyone who would listen. 'We would like to start from the beginning again and encourage people to question beliefs they have always held − principles which tie them to the world as it *is* rather than to the world as it *could be*. The aim will be to throw off the past and look to the future.'

He went on to describe the society growing and developing, becoming well known as a place where talented people of all races could think and work without worrying about financial, political or other problems. From small beginnings a city and later a nation would grow. Brilliant men and women would be tempted to the new nation by the opportunities for thinking and working; in would come the future Einsteins, Newtons and Curies.* One day, perhaps, it could become the place in which all great ideas were born . . . and of course Frederick, First Baron Foxfield would have succeeded in his goal of being remembered.

◆

It was my sister who invited me to dinner to meet Walter. By this time he was already trying to find suitable men and women to be involved in the Project. Looking back now, I am not greatly surprised that he was finding this difficult. In 'normal' circumstances I would almost certainly see someone like him as crazy. But when he spoke that evening, I felt myself beginning to share his enthusiasm. During the night I realized that I was excited at the thought of leaving behind the problems and worries of the present and helping to build a clean new world in a clean new place.

The next day I rang Walter and arranged to meet him again. From that moment I was a member of the Project team. Very soon afterwards, Walter took me to meet Lord Foxfield.

'Walter here has explained the main parts of the plan, so you'll

---

* Famous scientists of the past.

know that the idea is to begin with a small group of people who will be joined by others later. I have been finding out about you, Mr Delgrange,' Foxfield went on. 'I found your two books interesting. As a social historian you are trained to observe changes in society. This training will be very useful to the Project; we hope you will be able to help make decisions about the best ways of organizing our society and prevent the development of less satisfactory forms of organization.'

He continued in this way for some time, and I realized by the end of the evening that I now had the job of preparing a document that listed the laws of the new society and the rights of its citizens! It kept me busy for months.

As the weeks passed, Walter had great difficulty finding suitable people for the original group. He was disappointed by those who wanted to go, and began to feel that he was expecting too much. I did my best to interest some of my friends in the Project but, although they were sympathetic to the idea, none of them wished actually to be part of it. Soon after that, Walter disappeared for some time in search of a home for the Project. When he returned, he refused to say anything about the areas that he had been looking at except that one of them seemed just right. It was clear that things were beginning to happen. Lord Foxfield had opened a Project office, and a number of staff were working on the preparations.

I was left almost alone to develop my plans for the organization of the new society, and I was surprised and pleased to discover that Lord Foxfield allowed me considerable freedom in this.

◆

Then came the evening when Lord Foxfield told me: 'It's happened. We've got the place. It was all signed today.'

We drank to the long, successful life of the Project.

'And now, at last, may I know where it is?' I asked.

'It is an island called Tanakuatua,' he said. It was the first time I heard the name, and he said it as Tanner-kooer-tooer instead of Tanna-kwah-twah as we came to know it.

'Oh,' I said, 'Where is it?'

'It's just south-east of the Midsummers,' he explained.

The Midsummers meant nothing to me at the time – except that I had an idea they were somewhere on the other side of the world.

After that meeting, the Project became real in a new sense. The speed of preparation increased. I found myself becoming involved in meeting those who wished to be part of the group. Neither Walter nor I was happy about the quality of person – and we came to realize that the Project was attractive to those who found it difficult to fit into the society they wanted to leave. They saw themselves as escaping from their past lives rather than creating something new. At last, however, we were able to choose forty-six people to form the original group.

The newspapers began writing about the Project. At first they wanted to know how the British Government was able to sell a British-owned island to private interests. In the end, though, Lord Foxfield's power, and in particular his friendship with other newspaper owners, prevented any embarrassing public discussions about the sale. Instead, the papers wrote about the Project itself as the rather foolish idea of an old man, and about those involved as people who were not responsible enough to live in a normal, ordered society. We all found this time rather difficult, and five of our group changed their minds and decided not to go.

Chapter 2   A Strange Collection of People

On the evening before we left for the island, we gathered for dinner in a hotel in Bloomsbury. Most of us had never met before, and people looked at each other rather cautiously. Walter and I did our best to introduce everyone, but the atmosphere remained uncomfortable for some time.

Dinner and drinks helped a little, and at the end of the meal Lord Foxfield stood up to make a short speech.

'God,' began Lord Foxfield, rather surprisingly for him, 'God created man to be like him. He gave us the power to be the strongest of all living things on this earth. If God made us to be like him, it follows that he wanted men to become like God. This view is not new. Throughout history, leaders of nations have seen themselves as gods. Unfortunately, they have understood this to mean that they should separate themselves from other people. They were mistaken. We must *all* share the responsibility of organizing ourselves, and use our power to create a world that is sane and healthy. We can change society to meet our needs. We have become able to order society so that we can live side by side with nature without destroying it. We must control our future. If we are afraid to become men like gods, we will be destroyed!

'You are leaving to plant a seed in a brave new world – to care for it until it produces fresh crops that can feed a new society which is free of the evil and foolishness that have been part of life since the beginning of time.'

There was a lot more of this, and Lord F spoke with great confidence. To many people his words were slightly confusing, but by the end of the speech his message was clear:

'The knowledge and power to create a sane society exist. Here is your opportunity to use them. Now go out and do it. Good luck to you!'

♦

At the end of the meal Lord Foxfield stood up to make a short speech.

A colour photograph exists of our party gathered the next day on the *Susannah Dingley*. It was taken just before she sailed. By then our number had fallen to thirty-eight, and we were a strange collection of people. Nobody looking at the photograph would imagine that this group was going to plant the seeds of a new tomorrow on the other side of the world. And if luck had been with us, perhaps . . .

Mrs Brinkley is immediately noticeable on the left because she is holding a huge travel bag. Even without this bag you would notice her first because of her broad figure. One feels that, whatever the hopes of the rest of us may be, Deborah Brinkley knows exactly what she wants: it is more babies, and she is ready to go on having them in Tanakuatua or wherever else life may take her. This, and the sight of her strong, capable husband beside her, makes her the most confident-looking person in the group. Alicia Hardy stands next to them, talking to one of the Brinkley children.

But there can be no doubt that it is Marilyn Slaight (Mrs Slaight) who *thinks* she is the centre of attention. She looks like a model from a fashion magazine, dressed in the most unsuitable clothes imaginable for such a trip and with a great big smile for all the world. She stands next to Horace Tupple, his fat, babyish face looking out from above a beach shirt. Horace was the life of any party – and perhaps he found one in Panama, for that is where he decided to leave the ship and make his way home two weeks later. Sometimes it is surprising how wise a fool can be.

The small man in the front wearing the hat and looking terribly serious is Joe Shuttleshaw, a useful carpenter but by nature a rather angry man. Beside him is his wife Diane and beyond her Jennifer Felling, the nurse. The other Jennifer, Jennifer Deeds, looks calm and happy.

Walter Tirrie is there, of course. He is standing at a little distance from the rest of us. He is clearly the leader, and looks at the camera with great confidence.

James McIngoe, the engineer, is smiling on the right of the picture. Camilla Cogent stands next to him. She seems a lonely figure – there, but not with us. Her eyes are not on the camera, and she looks lost in thought.

I, Arnold Delgrange, am at the back, looking into the distance with an excited expression on my face. Even now I can remember my feelings at the time. I was about to sail, not on the *Susannah Dingley* but on a new *Argo.*★ As I look thoughtfully into the waters of the Thames, it is not London's dirty river that I see but the shining waters of the Aegean – and a distant island in which a lost world will be born again. How little I knew!

There we stand: Tom Conning, Jeremy Brandon, David Kamp and all the rest. All kinds of us, from Arnold Delgrange, the dreamer, to Charles Brinkley, the farmer. It is a sad photograph. We may not look much, but each of us was then filled with high hopes. And the idea that had brought us together was much greater than ourselves.

Ah, well, it will be tried again, I suppose. Men have been searching for freedom for thousands of years . . . Yes, they will try again – and the next time I hope luck will be with them.

Chapter 3   Tanakuatua

So we sailed for Tanakuatua.

When the *Susannah Dingley* left, I knew nothing of Tanakuatua except that it was a small island in the middle of the Pacific Ocean with nobody living on it. We had seen a few

★ A ship in a Greek legend, used by Jason and his followers on a long journey full of adventures.

pictures in old books, but these always showed the same view: a line of curving white beach in front of thick greenery and trees. Only the twin hills, Monu and Rana, rising behind the beach, make these pictures of Tanakuatua different from those of a thousand other islands. Both of the hills are, in fact, volcanoes – but neither appeared to have shown life for thousands of years.

We knew so little about the island before we left. Since then, I have been able to find out more about the history of the place, and my new knowledge allows me to understand only too well why this beautiful green island had nobody living on it, and how it came to be available to a private buyer. But more of that later.

◆

Our journey went smoothly. The only unexpected event was Horace Tupple's departure from the ship at Panama. The group showed very little interest in his attempts to lighten our spirits by organizing games and competitions, and by the time we were in the middle of the Atlantic, he was quite sure he had made a mistake in coming. The night before we reached Colón, he got drunk and told us all what he thought of us and the Project. The next day he walked off.

Poor Horace. Lucky Horace!

I tried to get to know my companions during the journey. For the first time since the accident I began to see people as individuals again. I had a sense of slowly waking – of coming back to life – and I began to see the Project as real. But together with this waking came a feeling of alarm similar to that which I imagine to follow a loss of memory.

I felt my companions changing little by little from shadowy figures into living people – and into different people from those I had expected them to be. And, perhaps, now we were on our way, they did change in certain ways . . . All I can be sure of is that *I* changed and that I saw them differently. The journey

10

cleared my mind, but with effects that were in some ways a little worrying.

For example, I came to realize that although we shared an idea about the aims of the Project, we had very different views on how these aims would be reached. Perhaps the building of this society would not be as smooth as I had thought. As I came back to the real world, my judgement began to return. It became clear to me that our intentions were very general, and we had not given much thought to how we would handle problems and disagreements. I recognized the need for the group to agree on how such matters would be managed.

My attempts to talk to Walter about this were not helpful. His view was that the developing society would create its rules when they became necessary and not before. He refused to listen to my arguments, and after a few more attempts I gave up. As the journey continued, I felt Walter becoming a different person. He was difficult to talk to and spent a lot of time away from the rest of us. The only person who could get close to him was Alicia Hardy; she seemed to be taking on the position of his private secretary.

I found it easier to get to know my other companions and their reasons for being part of the Project. Charles Brinkley wanted to be left alone to farm as he thought best, without the rules and resulting paperwork which made farming at home so difficult. Joe Shuttleshaw wanted his children to grow up in a free society away from the damaging class system at home. Others had their reasons – some caused by romanticism, some by unhappiness with their past lives. In fact, by the end of our journey I understood why most of our group had decided to join the Project. It was only Camilla Cogent who I found difficult to understand. She was not easy to talk to and always had a distant look in her eyes.

'I wanted to be useful,' she replied to my question. 'And as a biologist, I am naturally interested in the idea of an island that has had no people living on it for the last twenty years.'

Later in our journey I did succeed in having a deeper conversation with her. I learned that she was a doctor of biology and was a specialist in the study of insects – particularly those that cause damage to plants. She had worked in West Africa and on an island in the Indian Ocean, but had spent the last year at home. She did not speak about this last year and I suspected that something had happened – perhaps in her emotional life – which was causing her pain. I began to understand why Walter had chosen her, though; when she talked about her subject, she seemed to come to life, and there was no question that she was knowledgeable and capable.

Our last stop before Tanakuatua was Uijanji (We-yan-ye), the capital and the only port of the Midsummers. We stayed there for two days and left with a party of some twenty islanders to help with the landing of our luggage on Tanakuatua.

Camilla was surprised that we managed to get any islanders to come with us. She had spent the time on Uijanji talking to people, trying to find out as much as she could about Tanakuatua. The stories they told gave her plenty to think about.

'From what I have heard, there is a curse on the place' she told me. 'Any local person who is willing to go there is taking a great risk – especially if they refuse to believe in the curse.'

♦

Two days later we arrived.

Photographs had prepared me for the shape of Tanakuatua, but not for its colour. The bright blue of the sky was divided from the clear blues and greens of the sea by the island itself. Above the white beach there was a line of green, and beyond that the two hills, green below and blue-brown at the top. At first it seemed to me impossible that such a beautiful island had no people living on it. My second thought, though, was that it looked too good to be true.

As we approached the island, a few birds rose into the air with loud cries. Camilla looked at them, obviously puzzled, and said, more to herself than to me:

'Strange, so few birds . . . I expected far more birds . . .'

The islanders, following an idea of Walter's, made a raft from our larger containers and floated all our bags and boxes to the shore. When they arrived on the beach, the islanders ran to the edge of the trees, taking no notice of Walter's attempts to call them back. Following their leader, they went down on their knees and lowered their faces to the sand.

'What are they doing that for?' Charles's son Peter asked Jennifer Deeds.

'I don't know,' she admitted. 'People have different ways in different places. Perhaps they think it's the polite thing to do when you arrive on an island. Or it's possible that they are praying to the spirits of the island, asking them not to be annoyed with us for coming here uninvited – and perhaps asking their permission to stay for a day or two. Some people take things like that more seriously than we do.'

The leader now appeared to be making a speech.

'You may well be right,' I agreed. 'I hope they're satisfied that they've got permission, or we'll have to do all the heavy work ourselves.'

They did indeed seem to be satisfied, because after twenty minutes the islanders returned to take the bags off the raft. Charles Brinkley arranged for some of the larger boxes to be piled up and covered as a temporary sleeping area. Mrs Brinkley organized the building of a field kitchen. Jamie McIngoe found places for the heavy equipment, including the tractor, and the rest of us did what we could until night fell. Then we returned to the ship.

The islanders made a raft and floated all our bags and boxes to the shore.

◆

After dinner, I found Camilla listening to the singing of the islanders. The song was sometimes cheerful but more often sad, and I wished I could understand the story it was telling.

When it came to an end, Camilla nodded her head towards the island. 'Well,' she asked, 'What do you think of it?'

'It's beautiful,' I said. 'But it's a little frightening. All those plants fighting each other for existence. And *we've* got to fight them. I've been imagining the island as it will be later, I suppose. Is it what *you* expected?'

'Yes, I think so. Except for the birds . . . I don't understand that. There ought to be millions of birds.' She paused, considering. 'There seem to be very few flowers too.'

'But it's much as you would expect of a place without any people to upset nature's development?' I asked.

'People don't upset nature,' she answered. 'They are themselves children of nature. Anyway, nature is continuously changing – it never stands still. And no animal or plant has a *right* to exist. Even human beings may disappear or become something very different. Personally, I can't see much future for people unless we discover ways of changing ourselves.'

'Well let's hope that Lord F's Project succeeds, and that the discoveries are made here,' I said.

'You really believe in the dream, don't you?' she remarked.

'I believe in it as a possibility. Why not? This Project could succeed and become a powerful centre of knowledge in a way that democracy will never allow.'

We continued talking for an hour or more as the moon rose higher. In my mind I saw planted fields on the island, wide roads, and handsome buildings in which great discoveries were being made.

15

Chapter 4   The Project Begins

It took us five long days to carry everything to the shore, but it was done at last. We said goodbye to the crew of the *Susannah Dingley,* and watched the ship disappear into the distance. She would return in six months with more equipment and, we hoped, people, but until then we were on our own.

We all, adults and children, had a strong feeling of being alone. We looked at each other as if for the first time, as we realized that we now depended on each other. To me the island now became more active — a force we had to defeat. I did not believe in the curse, but I had the feeling that the island was thinking . . . waiting.

Charles sensed our mood and called us together. He took us to the place where he and Walter had decided that our settlement should be, and he explained how it would look. His confidence made us more cheerful, and we returned to the temporary home we had built, feeling enthusiastic and capable.

Walter read out the messages that he planned to send to Lord Foxfield and our families. We agreed that they were suitable, and Henry Slaight took them to the radio to send. He quickly returned, however, and whispered to Walter. Walter looked worried. I followed them back to the radio and saw that one of the heavy boxes had fallen onto the radio. When the box was lifted off, it was obvious that the radio was beyond repair.

'It can't just have fallen,' said Walter, looking up at the tidy wall of boxes. 'But who . . .? It would have needed two or three men to push the box down.' He shook his head in puzzlement. 'We'd better not tell the others for the moment.'

The next day we started work. Charles cleared the ground while Tom Conning, on the tractor, carried the materials to the place where we were starting to build. Henry Slaight arranged for power to operate lights in our huts, our temporary homes.

Mrs Brinkley organized the cooking. Jamie McIngoe went to look for a way to bring water to the settlement. Joe Shuttleshaw and some helpers prepared the parts of buildings that we had brought with us, so that we could move them into place when needed. Everybody, including the children, was given a job of some kind.

It went on like this for six days – leaving us all exhausted at the end of each. But by then Charles had cleared the ground and was preparing more land for planting. Building had begun, and water had begun to reach us through temporary pipes. We were pleased with our progress and when Walter said that we could have a day of rest, we felt that we had earned it.

We wondered how to spend our day off. Tom Conning, however, had no doubts.

'It's time we saw something of the place. It's nearly two weeks since we landed, and so far nobody's been more than a quarter of a mile from here. Would anyone like to climb the mountain with me for a view of the island?'

Alicia Hardy and four of the younger ones immediately accepted the invitation. Joe Shuttleshaw's son Andrew held up his hand too. When his father pulled it down again, he protested loudly.

'Let him come, Joe. He'll be no trouble,' Tom said.

I looked at Camilla.

'Not you? I thought you were keen to see more of the island.'

'I've got another idea. If Walter will let me have the small boat, we could go round the coast and perhaps land in a few places.'

◆

We got the boat. After saying goodbye to those climbing the mountain, and leaving most of the others lying around resting near the settlement, five of us set off round the island – Camilla, Jennifer Deeds, David Kamp, Jamie McIngoe and myself. We headed south round the point and then turned and made our way up the east coast. The coastline slowly changed from white beaches to dark cliffs. As we travelled, there was little conversation. Indeed, there was hardly any sound at all besides that of the waves moving against the side of the boat.

'But *why* are there no birds?' I heard Camilla ask herself under her breath.

Then I noticed something else. We could see clearly the trees immediately above us, but those in the distance at the top of the cliffs seemed to be covered with something white.

'What on earth's that?' I asked, pointing at the rocks. 'It looks like thick fog or something.'

Camilla raised her field glasses in the direction of my finger and studied the rocks carefully.

'I don't know. It doesn't seem to be moving at all, so it can't be fog. Can we get a little nearer?' she asked. 'It looks very strange. Perhaps it's some kind of tree disease.'

We moved the boat in a little closer. From this distance we could see the white stuff clearly. It looked quite solid.

'I must get some of that and examine it. Can you stop somewhere, Jamie?' asked Camilla.

Jamie pointed the boat towards the coast and found a place where the sand below the sea rose gently to the water's edge. As the sea became shallower, the front of the boat dug into the sand and came to a stop. Jamie turned off the engine.

The silence came down like a blanket.

'It's like the end of the world,' said Jennifer Deeds. Then she screamed. 'Look!' she said, pointing at something on the sand. 'It's moving!'

On the beach were half a dozen brown patches, each two to three feet across. One of them was sliding slowly along the beach in our direction.

'What is it? I don't like it,' Jennifer said nervously.

His head and shoulders were completely covered by one of the brown patches – it seemed to be moving.

As David Kamp got out of the boat and walked towards the brown patch to find out, others began to move. David reached the trees and put his hand up to touch the white stuff that covered them. Then something seemed to fall on him, hiding him from us, and suddenly there was a loud scream. David came running back towards the boat. His head and shoulders were completely covered by one of the brown patches – and it seemed to be moving. As he fell into the water, Jamie McIngoe and I jumped out to help him. The brown patch broke up into a thousand small pieces that floated off David and back towards the land. We saw his face. It was bright red. In alarm, we pulled him back into the boat. He was not breathing.

'He's dead,' Jennifer said. 'David's dead.'

Camilla had climbed over the side, but she returned now, carrying something in her handkerchief. She looked at David's face with great attention as Jennifer turned away.

Jamie broke the silence. 'We'd better go back,' he said, and started the engine.

'I know what that white stuff is,' said Camilla suddenly. 'It's a web. A spider's web.'

'But that's impossible,' I replied. 'All that web. It would take hundreds of millions of spiders . . .'

Camilla opened her handkerchief. Inside were half a dozen dead spiders. They were large and brown, but looked completely harmless.

'They're certainly spiders, and spiders like this are poisonous, but I'm not a specialist so I can't tell you much more about them. I do know that it would take two or three hundred bites at the same time to kill someone, and that's what's so strange.'

We looked at each other in silence.

Chapter 5   Spider Watching

I had hoped to talk to Walter or Charles about David's death before the others heard about it, but several people saw us arriving and came down to the shore to meet us. We covered the body in a blanket and carried it up the beach. Then Jamie and I went to look for Walter.

'Spiders!' he cried. 'What kind of spiders?'

We explained about the brown patches on the beach, and that hundreds of them must have dropped on David from the trees.

The three of us went to find Camilla. She was busy studying the dead spiders she had brought back.

'It seems impossible,' Walter said to her. 'I've never heard of spiders behaving like that.'

'That's what worries me,' Camilla agreed. 'Spiders *don't* behave like that. In fact they don't do anything at all as a group.'

Walter remained silent for a moment. 'The people who went up the mountain haven't returned yet,' he said.

When the sun went down, the explorers had still not returned and everyone was worried, especially Joe Shuttleshaw. He wanted to go and look for them but was persuaded that it would be dangerous to set off in the dark. We sat around the fire and waited.

'Why would it be dangerous?' one of the children asked. We hadn't told them about David's death. 'Is it because of the black men?'

'No,' Charles replied, puzzled. 'Why should you think that? They were perfectly harmless, and anyway they went back on the ship.'

'Then the black men we saw today must have been different ones,' Chloe continued. 'We saw them coming out of the trees this afternoon.'

'What? How many of them?'

'Only two. And they disappeared again quickly.'

We sat thoughtfully for a moment. Then Jamie put the question which was in everyone's mind.

'If some of the men who came with us have stayed here,' he said, 'what could their reason be?'

The question remained unanswered.

♦

We buried David in the morning, and Charles said a short prayer. The exploring group had still not returned.

Joe Shuttleshaw continued to demand a search-party, but nobody wanted to go with him. As Walter said, there were seven of them and anything that had harmed those seven might also harm another group of seven or more. The best thing to do for the moment was to continue working.

It was Camilla who suggested a solution.

'Joe's right,' she told Walter. 'We can't simply do nothing. I've got an idea – have we got any insecticide?'

By midday she and Joe were prepared. They put on long-sleeved jackets and gloves, and wore their trousers inside high boots. On their heads were wide hats, and over these were nets which covered their heads and were pushed into the tops of their jackets. They carried insecticide, and they had also poured some over their clothes.

'Insecticide is not likely to harm spiders,' Camilla said, 'but they won't like it, so they may keep away from us.'

As they were about to leave, Charles gave Camilla a gun.

'Can you use one of these?' he asked.

'Yes, but . . .'

'Then you'd better take it. After all, we're not *sure* spiders are the only trouble, are we? But be careful with it; we may need it later.'

About four hours later Camilla returned. She was walking slowly, carrying her hat and the net in her hand.

'Where's Joe?' Mrs Shuttleshaw cried.

'Did you find them?' asked Walter at the same time.

'Joe's coming,' Camilla answered. 'Yes . . . we found them . . .'

From the look on her face, it was obvious to everyone what she meant. She looked terrible, so while Walter tried to calm the others, I took her away and gave her a drink. Walter joined us.

'There were millions of spiders, climbing all over them,' Camilla told us quietly. It was clear from her voice and her eyes that she was in shock. 'Joe wanted to find his son. He started pouring insecticide over them. It was horrible, so I left.'

'They didn't attack you?' Walter asked.

'They tried,' she said. 'They came towards us and started to climb up our legs, but they didn't like the insecticide so they soon fell off. Some of them dropped on us from the trees, but they fell off too. They kept on trying. Hundreds of thousands of them. The others had no chance. It must have been quick – as it was with David . . .

There was a sound of voices outside, and I went to look. A figure was approaching, carrying something in his arms. As he came closer, I realized it was Joe. He was holding his son, Andrew, though the boy's awful injuries made him almost unrecognizable.

I poured Camilla another drink, and then we went to join the

Andrew Shuttleshaw was being buried while Joe sat on a fallen tree.
His wife had her arms around him.

others. Andrew Shuttleshaw was being buried while Joe sat on a fallen tree. His face was without expression; his eyes were fixed on a point straight in front of him but it was clear that he saw nothing. His wife had her arms around him and tears were running down her face. The rest of the group stood in silent horror.

In the evening, Joe Shuttleshaw, his wife and a few others called on Walter to say that they wished to leave the Project. They demanded that he send a message to the ship to come back and pick them up.

Walter was forced to tell them about the damage to the radio, but Joe lost his temper and refused to believe him until he was taken to see it for himself. In his anger he then accused Walter of damaging it on purpose to stop anyone leaving, and Charles had to come in and give Walter support until everyone had calmed down.

The next morning Charles called a meeting to make the situation clear to everyone.

'If, when the ship returns, any of you want to leave, you are free to do so. But for the next six months we are on our own and we have to make the best of the situation.'

He looked carefully at the gathered group before continuing.

'The spiders seem to be no closer than a mile and a half away, so we are safe here for the moment. But they might come nearer, and we have no way of knowing how long it will take them to reach us. We must therefore finish the buildings and clear a piece of land around them as quickly as we can. Then we'll pour insecticide on the ground around the buildings, keep more ready, and watch the cleared area carefully, twenty-four hours a day.'

Charles also recommended that we should dress as Camilla and Joe had whenever we walked beyond the cleared land.

At the end of the day, Camilla came to look for me.

'Hello,' I said. 'I haven't seen you working. Where have you been all day?'

25

'Spider-watching,' she told me. 'Walter is annoyed with me because I went alone. Will you come with me tomorrow?'

I hesitated, but eventually agreed. Camilla helped me to make the clothes I needed to protect myself against the spiders, and the next morning we set off along the water's edge. We continued along the beach for a couple of miles, then began climbing up some low cliffs. As we climbed, the forest became thicker and our progress slowed because we had to cut our way through the plants and trees. Although we could see no sign of the web yet, Camilla suggested we put on our hats and pour the insecticide over each other.

'As far as I can tell,' said Camilla, 'the spiders are gradually taking over the whole island, but we need to know how fast they're making progress. Then we'll be able to work out how much time we have before they reach the settlement. Or whether perhaps we should move further north so that we have more time before they reach us.'

'That would be difficult,' I replied. 'We can't move far from our luggage. But it would be useful to know when they're likely to attack, because then at least we could be properly prepared.'

We climbed a little further and at last came out of the forest on to a clear patch of higher rock. It gave us the best view we had yet had of the coast in front of us and of the south end of the two hills. We sat down and looked at the view, filled with amazement.

The area covered by the web began so gradually that it was almost impossible to see the edge of it. What we could see quite clearly, though, was that the part of the island which stretched from just behind the coastline to about halfway up the hillside was completely covered by web so thick that we could not see through it from where we were sitting. It must have taken millions and millions of spiders to make so much of it.

We continued up the hillside and quite soon met the first groups of spiders, although I did not notice them until they actually attacked. They came out of the trees to my left and surrounded my feet. I jumped in sudden fear.

'It's all right,' said Camilla, 'they won't hurt you.'

She was right. They climbed onto my boots and some of them started to run up my legs as far as the knees, but they suddenly lost interest, dropped off and ran away.

'Spiders smell, or taste with their feet – and they don't like the insecticide at all,' she said.

Soon we came out on another small area of clear ground overlooking a small beach on which we could see seven or eight familiar brown patches. I took out my glasses and looked more closely at each group. None of them was moving, and they all looked exactly the same. Then one group began to move.

'Look!' shouted Camilla. 'They're chasing that crab.'

The crab was on the beach near the line of trees and was running towards the sea. It went first one way, then another, in an attempt to avoid the groups of spiders. But whichever way it went, the spiders rushed to cut off its path to the water. Within a short time they had surrounded it. The crab tried to fight, but a few seconds later it had disappeared under a small mountain of spiders.

'That's interesting,' said Camilla. 'Did you notice that when the crab stopped, the spiders stopped too? They were confused when it stopped moving.'

♦

It was nearly eleven o'clock and I was hungry. We sat down and ate but kept watch for further events on the beach. Suddenly Camilla reached for her glasses. I looked in the direction she was pointing them and saw a thin column rising from the white of the web. I too picked up my glasses and noticed other, similar columns, like steam against the blue sky.

'What are those?' I asked Camilla.

'Millions of baby spiders,' she replied, 'setting out into the world. Carried up by the air as they hang from their webs in the tree-tops.'

I could hardly believe what she was saying. 'But they'll come down in the sea,' I said.

'Most of them will,' Camilla answered. 'But not all. Some of them will live.'

As she stopped speaking, I noticed a group of spiders coming towards us. Camilla saw that I was about to get up.

'Don't move,' she said, 'and they won't notice us. Remember the crab.'

There must have been three or four hundred spiders in the group, and we were sitting directly in their path. Just before they reached us, the whole group turned to the left and walked around our boots, then turned to the right and continued on their way. I breathed again, and Camilla picked up her glasses.

'They've found some eggs,' she said. 'There's so little for them to eat now on the island – except each other. How long will it be, I wonder, before they learn to catch fish?'

'Or build boats?' I suggested.

'No, I'm serious. They learnt to build webs in order to catch flies. The same stuff could be made into nets to catch fish, and in fact, from what we've seen, I think it's very likely. These spiders, unlike others, have found a need to change, and it's their *way of behaving* that has changed rather than their appearance. Most spiders don't look for food together or share it when they find it. What we're seeing here is an amazing development.'

We covered ourselves with insecticide once again, and set out on the return journey. As we walked we were attacked again and

28

again by spiders which climbed to our knees but then dropped to the ground.

We stopped for a moment beside a stream, and my eyes followed Camilla's pointing finger. On the other side of the stream, among the rocks, was a group of spiders which seemed to be doing nothing. Then the light caught the string of a web, carried slowly across the stream by the air. Suddenly a spider ran to the bank, threw itself on to the string and used it to cross the stream. Other spiders followed and the web grew thicker until it formed a definite bridge.

'Perhaps Charles's plan for an area of cleared ground is not as useful as we thought,' Camilla said as we walked on thoughtfully.

We observed one more thing of interest on our way back. Lying beside our path was a large rat – at least it *had* been a large rat; now it was just dry skin, and bones picked quite clean. We looked at it for some time without speaking.

Chapter 6   Prisoners

That evening we told Walter and Charles what we had seen. Charles was worried by our story of the spiders crossing the stream, but pointed out that the wind would need to be in the right direction for them to cross our clearing and that we could watch particularly carefully at those times.

'Yes, but there aren't enough of us to guard the whole area if the spiders come in their thousands,' Camilla said.

Charles nodded. 'We must clear more land,' he agreed, 'so that it will be too far for the wind to carry the webs and allow the spiders to begin their bridge. We'll burn the trees down.'

It was decided that Camilla and I would go out the next day and begin cutting a path across the island, so that we could then start fires along it.

'I'm sorry the two of you will have to go alone,' Charles said. 'I need the others to finish the main buildings. Everyone will feel much safer when they know there's somewhere they can go if the spiders attack.'

There was a slight smile at the corners of Camilla's mouth. 'What you really mean is that nobody else will go near the spiders!'

She turned to me. 'What about you, Arnold? How do you feel about going?'

'I wasn't exactly enthusiastic this morning,' I admitted, 'but it's been an educational day as far as getting to know our enemy is concerned. Yes, I'll come.'

♦

We set off again early the next morning, dressed as we had been the day before. We had walked for over an hour along the narrow path cut by the exploring party before the first group of spiders dropped onto Camilla's head – and fell off immediately as they came into contact with the insecticide. Having found the edge of their hunting ground, we walked back the way we had come for about twenty minutes until we found a place which would be suitable as the start of a fire line to the north.

We sat down for a moment and considered the difficult job of cutting through the plants and trees that surrounded us.

'I've been thinking,' Camilla said. 'We've already seen how powerful the spiders have become now that they co-operate with each other and have found new uses for their webs. Even in their war against *us,* it's the spiders

30

who took the first blood. Where will this lead, I wonder?'

'You don't seriously think they would be threatening anywhere else, do you? It's just that we're on a small island and don't have much to defeat them with.'

'But look how quickly these spiders have developed,' Camilla argued. 'They no longer have any natural enemies, so they're only limited by food. The search for food continues to drive them forward. And they're not just spiders now. They know as a group when to work or attack – just as bees do, but perhaps with even greater efficiency.'

'These are frightening ideas,' I said, standing up, 'and we've got a job to do. Shall we get started?'

For an hour we worked to clear a path, cutting down what we could and going round the larger trees. Then we sat down again for a rest.

I returned to our earlier conversation. 'But surely, when the spiders have eaten everything on the island, they'll all die. Some may live longer by eating others, but after that . . .'

'But perhaps they *will* learn to catch fish,' said Camilla. 'If they could do that, nothing could stop them.'

'But that's crazy. How can spiders catch fish?'

'Co-operation makes many things possible. Working together, they could make nets and stretch them across a small beach. Later they'd invent new methods of catching them.'

'But you talk as if spiders were able to think logically!' I complained.

'Well, it seems they have some kind of group intelligence. They're producing ideas to solve their group problems. They may not have intelligence as we know it, but they have something.'

Suddenly, two figures rushed towards us from out of the trees.
They were carrying long knives in their hands.

'Oh come on, Camilla. Surely what you're saying is an exaggeration. What we have here is an unusual situation in which one group has been able to multiply quickly. It will grow until its food is no longer available and will then die.'

'I hope you're right,' she replied.

We continued up the hill, until, to our great surprise, we found a path. We stopped and looked, first at each other and then each way along the path. At first there was only silence. Then, suddenly, two figures rushed towards us from out of the trees. They were carrying long knives in their hands. Before we knew what had happened, we were prisoners.

They searched us quickly and took away our own knives and Charles's gun. They wore no clothes except for small cloths around their waists, simple shoes, and belts from which were hanging knives of different shapes and sizes. The most noticeable thing about them, though, was that their dark skin was shining: from their feet to the top of their hair, they were covered in some kind of oil that had an extremely strong and unpleasantly sharp smell.

One of them put the knife he was holding back into his belt and looked carefully at the gun, smiling with satis- faction. He pointed it at us and made a sign for us to move. There was no arguing with that, so we began walking. As soon as we had turned the first bend in the path, we were ordered to stop. Beside the path were four large bags made of leaves, which Camilla looked at with interest. At first I couldn't understand why, but then I too noticed that the bags were moving.

'What . . .?' I was beginning, when the two men grabbed our arms and, before we could speak, tied our hands together. They then told us to keep quiet and continue walking.

Other islanders appeared, picked up three of the bags and walked in the opposite direction to us. The fourth bag remained at the side of the path. What bad luck to have met these people! They must have heard us cutting our way through the trees and stopped what they were doing to see what was happening. Now three of them were continuing with their business while the fourth led us straight into the heart of spider country.

◆

After a short time we met our first group of spiders.

'Stop!' shouted our guard.

The spiders ran towards us and climbed over our feet and up our legs. But, once again, they stopped at our knees and dropped off. The guard was watching carefully and seemed surprised. Then he said, 'Go on!'

I noticed that the spiders made no attempt to attack him; in fact they stopped before they even got to his feet and it was clear that the oil on his skin was keeping them away. As we continued, more and more groups of spiders appeared until we were attacked every few yards.

The path we were walking along was obviously an old path which had recently been cleared. I could see that it had been wider in the past and more used. The web was becoming thicker now, with large webs stretched between the trees. On each one was a group of spiders waiting patiently for food to pass by. I saw no other animals or insects anywhere, and it seemed unlikely that these groups would find anything to eat.

At last we came to an area where there were fewer spiders and broken webs hung like ghostly torn cloth from the branches of the trees. It seemed to me that some of the ghostly feeling was created by the fact that there was very little light. Looking up, I realized that we could not see the sky at all. We seemed to be in a huge tent stretched over the top of the forest. The spiders were higher now, and there were none on the ground nor in the lower branches. Nothing moved. The only sound was our footsteps on the forest floor.

The trees came to an end quite suddenly, and we came out of the forest on to an open hillside covered with a knee-high plant I did not recognize. This area was almost completely free of spiders and I wondered whether it was something to do with the plant.

We continued climbing up the side of Monu, the hill to the south, until we reached the lip of the old volcano. There we were told to sit down.

We had the best view of Tanakuatua that we had yet had – and it was a very strange view. About half the island was covered with the grey web, although a narrow piece of coast about a mile wide was clear around our settlement and along the west coast. In two or three places we could see the columns of what seemed to be steam rising up high into the sky. We looked down into the mouth of the volcano, at grass and, below that, a patch of bare rock which led down to a pool of boiling mud.

'It's easy to imagine this being a religious place. The volcano seems to be alive,' Camilla commented.

We continued to look down at the mud for some time, and our guard too seemed unable to take his eyes off the bottom of the volcano. After a time, however, he ordered us to stand up and walk around the lip of the volcano to where it met the other hill. As we walked, we passed an arrange-ment of stones, carefully placed to make a kind of table about three feet high. The top of it was covered in dark, dried blood.

We walked on. Suddenly our guard shouted something and two dark-skinned figures appeared on the path below us. Our hands were untied before the guard pushed us forward. The path was becoming difficult now, but eventually we reached the other two men. I recognized one of them at once. He had been noticeably older than the rest of the group we had picked up at Uijanji, and I remembered the grey in his hair. Without that I would not have known him now, dressed only in a cloth and with a bone through his nose.

But there was something else about him. A design was painted in yellow on his chest. Eight lines were drawn out from a circle in the centre, with small lines on the end of each. At first I did not understand the meaning of this picture, but then I noticed Camilla's face. I looked again. Of course . . . It was a spider . . .

Chapter 7   Naeta's Story

The man with the spider on his chest looked at us for a moment before turning to question our guard. Then he gave an order to his companion. The man stepped forward and took my bag. It would have been pointless to struggle. I let him have it.

They discovered the insecticide, smelt it, nodded and poured it on the ground. The other contents did not interest them. They searched Camilla's bag too, and poured away her insecticide.

The man with the spider came closer to us and smelt my sleeve.

'Take your clothes off,' he said, in English. 'Both of you.'

We hesitated, but our guard made a movement with his knife and we obeyed. We were allowed to keep on our underwear and shoes. The third man picked up our clothes and carried them into the trees. The man with the spider on his chest said something to our guard who, although obviously unwilling, gave him our gun and then left. He looked at us once more and then walked into the trees, leaving us alone.

We sat on the ground and thought about the situation.

After a while, Camilla shook her head. 'I don't understand it,' she said. 'Why didn't they just kill us? It would be so easy.'

'Why are they here at all?' I replied.

'And why are they carrying spiders around in their bags? I'm sure they *are* spiders – the contents were moving,' Camilla continued.

We considered this, and then picked up our bags and ate a sandwich and a bar of chocolate that were in them. After that there was nothing to do.

As it grew dark, we decided to collect branches and leaves and build some cover for the night. We sat under this rough roof and watched through the trees the light of a fire that the two islanders had build. When some time had passed, Camilla stood up.

'I'm going to get warm by that fire,' she said firmly, and walked off towards it, taking no notice of my protests.

The islanders must have heard us, but they made no sign as we approached and then sat down beside the fire. The silence was eventually broken by the man with grey hair.

'Why did you come to Tanakuatua?' he asked.

'Why are *you* here?' Camilla replied. 'Isn't Tanakuatua forbidden to you? It isn't to us.'

37

'Tanakuatua is forbidden to all men and women,' he said. 'We came
only to help the Little Sisters.'

'Tanakuatua is forbidden to all men and women. We came only to help the Little Sisters. That is allowed. Tanakuatua is our island, *our* home, *ours*. It was taken from us by a trick.'

Camilla looked interested.

'What was this trick?' she asked.

The man did not reply at once. He looked at us both as if making up his mind. Then he decided to tell the story.

♦

'I am Naeta, son of Nokiki. It was in the time of my father . . . ' he began and, with emotion in his voice, this – as I remember it now – is what he told us.

Many years ago, at the beginning of this century, Tanakuatua was taken by the British for King George V. For a time there were soldiers on the island, but then they were taken away and island life returned to normal except for occasional visits by the Governor of the region.

Much later, during the 1939–45 War, soldiers returned to the island, but the Tanakuatuans were treated by the officers as its true owners, and relations remained good until the time when the island no longer needed protection and the soldiers left again.

Three years passed, and then the Governor arrived on one of his visits. He told the Tanakuatuans that something was going to happen to the east of the island, A great ball of fire, brighter than a hundred suns, would rise from the ocean. It would be so hot that trees would be burnt and the eyes of anyone who saw it would be damaged. After the fire ball had died, it would leave poison dust in the air which would kill any person it fell on.

It was hoped, he went on, that none of this dust would fall on Tanakuatua, but no one could control the winds and there was a small possibility that it would reach the island. So the King, concerned for his people, had ordered that the islanders should leave their homes for a short time and go to a place where they would be out of danger. The islanders would of course receive money for losing their homes and their crops.

The news was received quietly, because the islanders were too shocked to believe that they had heard correctly.

A meeting of the older men was called by the chief, Tatake. Most people were too confused to say much, so the discussion developed between Tatake himself and Nokiki, the head medicine man.

'We cannot accept this,' Nokiki argued. 'We must call on the young men to fight.'

'The young men will not fight,' replied Tatake. 'The men are brave, but this is not good sense. They cannot win against guns, and we must remain strong for the day we return to the island.'

Nokiki did not believe this talk of return.

'Who is this king that no one ever sees?' he asked. 'He lies to us because he wants our land. Better to be killed on Tanakuatua than to live as cowards.'

The great discussion continued through the night, and neither man could persuade the other. A month passed, three-quarters of the islanders supporting the chief, the rest the medicine man.

When the Governor returned, the Tanakuatuans seemed to be prepared. They started carrying their things onto the boat. The governor was pleased, and praised Tatake.

'Have you checked that everyone is here?' he asked.

'Nokiki will not come. And eighty of my people. They will stay. They swear it,' Tatake answered dully. 'Nokiki says they will fight.'

'Nonsense!' said the Governor. 'The order was clear. They must leave.' He turned to speak to a young man beside him, telling him to go immediately to the village.

The young man failed to persuade the rebels, and so police were sent in. Gunfire was heard, and then the police returned with a number of frightened-looking islanders. Tatake counted them and reported that there were probably about half a dozen left with Nokiki.

The Governor was angry, but was not prepared to wait any longer.

'I've warned them,' he said, and walked to the ship. Half an hour later, the ship left with Tanakuatuans looking silently back at the island home they were leaving behind.

After the departure of the ship, Nokiki continued to sit on the beach, looking out over the wide empty ocean. He did not speak, nor did he seem to notice his wife or the other three who had stayed behind. Soon they went off in search of food and left him sitting alone. Night fell, but still Nokiki did not move.

He thought of the past and of the proud history of his people. He remembered the traditional ways that had been so important before their first meeting with the white man. They had wandered across the ocean, fighting, settling on islands, setting off again, searching for the lost paradise.

The arrival of the white man had gradually changed the way of life of his people. They became confused by foreign habits and began to forget their own. They lost respect for the traditional ways. Was it any surprise that the spirits of their fathers should be offended?

Nokiki decided that it had been the capture of Tanakuatua by his own people that had been the beginning of the end. They had arrived in traditional style, defeated those already on the island and then made it their home. Ever since that time, it seemed that some evil on the island had made his people weaker and less proud. Now they were reduced to the frightened creatures he had seen being led like sheep to the ship earlier that day. The moon shone on Nokiki's cheeks. It shone on tears of shame and anger for a world that had gone. He knew what he had to do.

The following day, Nokiki prepared himself. He was already

41

wearing his finest bone decorations, and the others helped him paint his body red and white in the traditional way. Last of all, the woman drew in red on his chest the spider sign of his people. That finished, he put on strings of teeth and bones, and a belt into which he placed a long knife. Then he walked from the hut and led the way towards the two hills.

At a point where the two hills met, he chose a place and ordered the others to build an altar. By midday the altar was finished and Nokiki began to dig a hole beside it, not letting the others help him.

That night the others slept, but Nokiki did not. He sat as he had the night before, in silence, looking out over the ocean, thinking about his people's past.

A little before dawn, he stood up and moved to the altar, placed offerings on it and waited for the coming of Au, god of the Rising Sun. As the first light from the sun lit the high clouds, he began a low song which woke the others. They sat up and watched quietly.

Nokiki turned to the rising sun before beginning his work. Then he started. He cursed the island of Tanakuatua for destroying his people. He cursed it from north to south, from east to west, from the top of the hills to the water's edge. He cursed the ground and the rocks, its fruits and trees, all that ran on it or flew over it. He cursed it by day and by night – in the dry season, in the rainy season.

The others had never heard such a deep, terrible curse and it frightened them greatly. But Nokiki was not finished. He asked Nakaa, the highest god of all, to make Tanakuatua for ever forbidden to all people; he asked that any who tried to live in Tanakuatua should die horrible deaths, and when the ghosts of such people came to be judged that they should be refused entrance to the Happy Land.

Nokiki was finished now. He stood completely still, arms by

his side, and looked directly into the sun for a full minute. Then, suddenly and rapidly, he pulled the knife from his belt and drove it deep into his chest. He remained standing for a moment, then fell forward across the altar.

They wrapped him in leaves and buried him in the hole he had dug, before leaving the island as fast as they could.

Six months later, inspectors reported that in fact little of the poison dust had reached the island, but that it would not be completely safe for the islanders to return for about five years.

It was nearly ten years, however, before the Tanakuatuans were told that a ship would now take them home. But the four who had remained with Nokiki had brought news of the curse, and none but a few of the young men wanted to go.

'Nakaa does not forgive,' Tatake told the District Officer. 'When he has judged, he has judged. Tanakuatua is forbidden to us. The Government must give us a new island, and we will move there.'

The Government eventually agreed. The islanders were paid a small amount of money, and were given land on the island where they had been living for the past ten years.

The fields on Tanakuatua became wild again; and the houses fell down and became covered by the forest. No one visited the island, and it remained almost forgotten until news came that a white man was flying in to have a look. He decided to buy it. Shortly afterwards, the Government sold it to him for £30,000.

♦

We had sat silently through the telling of the story, but as Naeta finished, Camilla said, 'But surely it was sensible of you to sell an island that you couldn't live on.'

Naeta became angry. 'We did not sell. Tanakuatua is ours,' he replied. 'The Government tricked us by selling what was not theirs to sell. The curse was their fault in the first place, and they then made a profit by selling our true home.'

Naeta went on to explain to us that he was one of the four who had remained on the island until his father's death. He had since become the head medicine man and knew that although Nokiki's act had made Tanakuatua forbidden, it was also doubly religious for the people of the spider. He therefore had to act, and the opportunity came with the news that men were wanted to help a group of white people land on the island. Naeta had thanked the gods for showing him the way. He had called a meeting of his followers and explained his plan.

A lot of this confused us, but one thing was clear.

'So you made a decision to come to an island that was forbidden to you,' said Camilla. 'I don't understand that.'

Naeta nodded. 'Nakaa understands,' he answered. 'He knows that we come only to do his work. To help the Little Sisters. We do not come to live here. So we are safe. Now you tell me why you came here.'

'All right,' agreed Camilla, and she told him about the Project.

It was impossible to tell how much he understood of it, as he listened without expression, looking into the flames. Even to me, now, it sounded unreal – just a crazy dream.

'You knew about the curse,' Naeta said when Camilla had finished. 'You knew, but you did not care. It is foolish, very foolish. You did not know about the Little Sisters.'

'Who are these Little Sisters?'

Naeta touched the sign on his chest. 'Spiders are *my* little sisters,' he answered. 'Nakaa caused them to come from the dead body of my father. Therefore they are sisters, and brothers, to me.' He paused, and then went on. 'Nakaa has sent them to punish the world. Now they are only in Tanakuatua, but he has taught them how to fly. Already they are setting out on winds which will take them to all corners of the earth. They will carry the curse there, and that will be Nakaa's revenge.'

'I don't understand – revenge for what?' Camilla asked.

'When the white men came, many of our people stopped following Nakaa's laws. They were tested, and they failed. Nakaa watched them. He watched as fewer and fewer were able to enter the Happy Land, and when he heard my father's request, he made his decision. Not only the Happy Land, but also the world is forbidden to us now. Nakaa has ordered the Little Sisters to destroy the people.'

'But I still don't understand why you're here,' Camilla told him.

'Some of us still obey Nakaa's laws. We accept his judgement, and we shall do as he orders so that when we are judged, he will open the door for us. That is why we have come to help the Little Sisters. We have succeeded so far in giving them more time, by stopping you from asking for help which might have destroyed them.'

'So it was you who damaged the radio?' Camilla asked.

Naeta nodded. 'That was necessary,' he said. 'And now that I know why you have come, I understand why Nakaa wanted us to come here and help the Little Sisters.'

Naeta got up and, without saying any more, went into a small house of leaves and branches close by. I threw the remaining sticks on the fire, and Camilla and I lay down to get what sleep we could.

◆

I woke to see Naeta and the other man making a meal of some unpleasant-looking substance which they then ate from a tin. Camilla was also awake.

'I don't think I want any of that stuff,' she said, 'but I could do with a drink.'

She walked over and asked for some water. Naeta hesitated, but then passed her a petrol can of water.

'Now you go away,' he said. So we went, back to the place where we had left our bags, and ate our last two bars of chocolate. Then we looked at each other.

'Well, what do we do now?' Camilla asked. 'We might have a chance with our clothes, but I saw my belt in the fire.'

'Oh,' I said. 'Oh.'

We sat there for about an hour thinking about ways we could signal for help, and then we heard the islanders approaching. Their skins were shining now with oil, and there was a sharp smell as they passed by us without speaking. We watched them disappear; then we went back to the fire.

Among the tins that they had left behind, we found one which had the same sharp smell. It was empty.

'That must be the stuff they use to keep the spiders off,' I said.

'Yes, the smell reminds me of something,' Camilla replied. 'They must have pressed it from something. They would need some kind of rock basin. Let's see if we can find it.'

It took us twenty minutes to find the place, a natural basin with a channel down which the juice could flow. In the basin were the remains of the vegetable they had used.

'It's those plants on the hillsides that the spiders don't like,' Camilla said. 'Do you remember? Their webs hardly touched it.'

We spent the rest of the day collecting the plants and pressing them. It was tiring work, but by nightfall we had enough of the juice to protect ourselves on our walk back. That night we slept well.

46

The next morning we covered ourselves in the juice, collected our bags and set off on the return journey. Spiders came close to our feet, but then stopped and walked away.

'I think we're going to be all right as long as we don't meet any of the islanders,' Camilla said. 'I wonder how they learnt about this stuff.'

'If your sign is a spider, you probably know a lot about them,' I suggested. 'Anyway, it works, so let's hurry while it still does.'

We walked through the trees. The silence was frightening, and I would not have wanted to be there alone. Eventually we reached the place, on the edge of the spider region, where the webs were lower. A hundred yards further on we were free of them. From the place where the islanders had captured us, we took the path which we had cut through the forest.

♦

The first thing we saw when we reached the beach was our small boat out at sea. There was no one on the shore, and no reply to our shouts. Then, just in front of us, we noticed a brown patch. It began to move towards us.

'Oh, no – no!' cried Camilla.

I hurried on to the settlement, and looked into the room where the men had slept. It was difficult to see anything in the shadow at first. But then I did . . .

I turned away. I was able to take four or five steps before I was horribly sick. 'Don't go in there,' I shouted to Camilla, before being sick again.

When I had recovered, I found Camilla. A group of spiders was watching her, but she took no notice. In her hands was a small bag like those the islanders had been carrying. It was empty.

She looked at me, and I knew we were both remembering a similar bag that had lain beside the path, with contents that moved slightly.

'Now we understand what he meant by "helping the Little Sisters",' she said, unsteadily. 'Are they all . . .?'

I nodded. The silence and what I had seen left no doubt of it.

'They must have come in the night, and – oh, horrible, horrible.' For the first time since I had known her, she burst into tears.

The small boat was disappearing into the distance. The islanders were on their way, having done what they had to do.

Chapter 8   Rescued

It was about a week later that the aeroplane came; at least, I think it was – we were both beginning to lose our sense of time.

Camilla and I were just completing the first building, and trying to make it impossible for spiders to enter. We had thought about moving to another part of the island, but we didn't want to cut a new path and clear more ground. Anyway, carrying all our things very far was not practical, and we were sure the spiders would find us eventually.

During that week we lived on our nerves. The spiders were always there, watching and waiting. I began to have the feeling that they were prepared to sit there until the ring of insecticide we were using as a barrier lost its power, and that thousands of them would then pour across. Almost every day, they built a bridge and started coming over; we would have to stop whatever we were doing and attack them with the insecticide. We slept under nets, and checked the area every morning to see if any spiders had crossed the barrier.

We were busy dragging the rest of the boxes into the settlement with the help of the tractor, when suddenly I heard a cry from Camilla and turned to see her running towards me from the beach. She was pointing wildly at the open sea.

'Look, Arnold! Look out there!'

And there it was. A small plane was resting on the surface of the water, and beside it two figures were getting into a rubber boat. The noise of the tractor must have drowned the sound of their engines and prevented us from hearing them.

'Quick,' Camilla said, pulling me towards the beach. 'We must stop them from coming to shore.'

When we came out of the trees, the boat was already in shallow water and one of the men was stepping out. Camilla and I both shouted. They heard us and waved. We shouted again and waved them away, but it was no good. One of them had noticed the brown patch. He said something to his companion and bent down to look at it more closely. The patch reached his feet and then moved up his legs.

There was a scream.

The second man jumped forward to help him. In a moment the spiders were all over him. Then *he* screamed . . .

After a time, Camilla, looking across the water, asked, 'Can you fly a plane?'

'No,' I answered. 'Can you?'

'No,' she said.

We continued looking at the plane.

'There must be a radio on it,' she said, eventually.

We walked across to the boat, keeping our eyes away from the bodies, and made our way out to the plane. There was a radio, and a voice was coming from it, but we could

I pressed the switch marked 'Receive', but the voice continued.
I had no idea if anyone had heard me.

understand nothing. I pressed the switch marked 'Speak' and talked; then I pressed the one marked 'Receive', but the voice continued. I had no idea whether anyone had heard me or not.

Camilla tried too, but with no better result, so we took the boat back to the beach. We did at least feel that someone was worried enough about us to send a plane, and that they might try again when the plane did not return.

◆

Five days later, a ship arrived. A small boat set out from it to the plane and then towards us, where we were standing waving on the shore. There were four people in the boat, looking at us with amazement.

We took off our hats and nets, but they still looked confused.

'Are you Mr Tirrie?' one of them, an officer, asked.

'Tirrie is dead,' I answered. 'They're all dead except us.'

'It's the spiders,' Camilla added.

The man did not seem to find her explanation satisfactory. His eyes wandered to the two bodies on the beach. 'And those two?' he asked, looking back at us.

'The spiders got them. We tried to stop them . . . ' Camilla told him.

'The spiders,' he repeated, looking at her hard.

'Yes, there,' said Camilla, pointing to a brown patch on the sand.

The man sighed. 'I'd better have a look at them.' he said, getting to his feet.

'No!' cried Camilla. 'You don't understand. They'll kill you. Arnold, stop him!'

'The spiders?' the man said. It was clear that he thought we had some reason for not wanting him to look too closely at the bodies.

51

'Look,' I said, 'Why do you think we're dressed like this? At least be sensible and protect yourself.' I held my hat and gloves out to him.

He put them on as if he was trying to satisfy the peculiar wishes of a small child. Camilla tied the net around his neck, and pulled his socks over his trousers. The other men were smiling, but less confidently now.

We watched as the officer started walking up the beach. At least three groups of spiders noticed him and started towards him. The smiles disappeared completely from the other men's faces. One of them shouted and pointed, but the officer just waved and continued. As he bent over the bodies, the spiders reached him and poured up over him. The officer tried to knock them off, but they kept coming. For a moment he stood there, then he ran to the sea and threw himself in. It took three dives before they had all floated off. When we reached him in the boat, he was standing in the water, screaming.

'My arms,' he cried. 'Oh, God. My arms.'

We pulled off his jacket, and four or five spiders fell out. We killed them, but there were bright-red patches on his arms. We pulled him into the boat and set off for the ship.

Chapter 9   The End of the Little Sisters?

Well, that was the end of Lord F's Project. Camilla and I were interviewed by the army, of course, but it was difficult to persuade them of just how many spiders there had been, and that we had indeed done everything we could. Despite the suffering of their own officer, now in hospital, it was clear that everyone thought we were slightly mad.

After a number of equally unsatisfactory interviews, we were flown back to Tanakuatua. The sight of an island half-covered with web had an effect on our companions, and their manner towards us changed. While Camilla went off with a naturalist, I showed the others the bodies on the beach and inside. They began to look rather sick. I took them to our new building, which was now covered with spiders, and we stood watching them for a while.

'It looks to me,' said a man sent by Lord Foxfield, 'as if the only thing to do is to cover the whole island from the air with insecticide.'

'No good.' A man from the Foreign Office★ shook his head. 'It would just lie on that web. Why don't we just leave them alone until they're forced to eat each other?'

I explained Camilla's theory about them learning to catch fish. 'Besides,' I said, 'the longer we leave them, the more chance they have to spread.'

We were still discussing the possibilities when Camilla and the naturalist returned. They were carrying boxes full of spiders.

'The Little Sisters,' Camilla said. 'Named, for the moment, *Araneus nokikii*.'

The following day we flew home. Two days later we were telling our story to Lord Foxfield. He was very annoyed, and interrupted us with cries of 'Tch-Tch!,' 'Most unfortunate!' and even, occasionally, 'Terrible!'

'But surely,' he said at the end, 'surely there was something you could do to prevent this tragedy.'

'Perhaps,' replied Camilla, 'we were not quite as powerful as the gods.'

The interview ended with Lord Foxfield telling us that he believed that the island had been poisoned, that he had therefore been deceived by the Government, and that he would be taking them to court. We would, of course, be called as witnesses.

★ The Government department which deals with foreign relations.

Naturally enough, we were never called. The matter was settled out of court, and Lord Foxfield was given his money back for the island itself and for the cost of our transport and equipment. Payments were also made to the families of those who had died.

I do not know what steps were taken to get rid of the Little Sisters, but in any case the problem appeared to be solved when Tanakuatua erupted – if it did erupt. Reports from Tokyo, Moscow and San Francisco of bombs being tested were denied at the same time as the news of the eruption became public. There were, we were told, no longer any signs of life on Tanakuatua.

I still hear occasionally from Camilla; she seems to travel around the world a lot. Most of her letters contain newspaper stories of deaths from spider bites. Recently, though, she sent me a small box, posted from somewhere in Peru. Inside, in a bottle of spirit, was a single spider which I had no problem recognizing as a Little Sister – *Araneus nokikii*.

ACTIVITIES

Chapters 1–2

Before you read

1 Look at the pictures in this book. What do you think the story is about? Where do you think it takes place?
2 Check the word *project* in your dictionary. Which of the following words are similar in meaning to *project*?
   activity   broadcast   chapter   idea
   interview   job   opportunity   plan
3 Make sentences using these pairs of words:
   a project/manager
   b project/study

After you read

4 Answer these questions:
   a Why is the writer so enthusiastic about Lord Foxfield's Project?
   b Why is Lord Foxfield willing to support the Project?
   c How does the writer meet Walter Tirrie?
   d What is Delgrange's job as part of the Project?
   e They have difficulty finding suitable people to go in the original group. What sort of people are attracted to the idea?
   f Where do they all meet for the first time?
5 Match the descriptions to the people:
   a Camilla Cogent   calm and happy
   b Jennifer Deeds   large and confident-looking
   c Deborah Brinkley   strong and capable
   d Charles Brinkley   lonely and thoughtful
6 Explain the writer's feelings when the photo was taken.

Chapters 3–4

Before you read

7   Check these words in your dictionary and make sure you understand them.

biologist   cliff   patch   raft
tractor   volcano   web

Now put each word with another from the following list and make a
sentence using each pair. Use each word only once.

float   island   mend   overlook   spider   study   vehicle

8   Which of the characters do you think will find life on the island most
difficult?

9   How do you think the children in the group will manage?

After you read

10   Answer these questions:

   a   Why does Horace Tupple leave the Project?
   b   Why doesn't Walter listen to the writer's concerns about building the new society?
   c   Why has Camilla joined the group?
   d   What surprises Camilla as they approach the island?
   e   What are Camilla's first thoughts about the white stuff on the
trees?
   f   Who notices the spiders first?

11   Imagine the conversation between the writer and Camilla as their
boat approaches Tanakuatua and they see the island for the first
time. With another student, act out their conversation.

Chapters 5–6

Before you read

12   What do you think the group will do next?

13   Look at these words. If you don't understand them, check in your
dictionary.

crab   insecticide

Write a sentence for each word, to show their meanings clearly.

After you read

14 Are these sentences true or false?

    a Camilla thinks the spiders' behaviour is unusual.

    b The children saw two black men coming out of the trees that morning.

    c Joe gives Camilla a gun.

    d The spiders don't like the insecticide.

    e Walter tells Joe about the radio but he doesn't believe him.

15 With other students, role-play the conversation between some of the group and Walter, when they tell him they want to leave the island (page 25).

16 When they are captured, what do Arnold and Camilla notice first about the two men?

17 What is strange about the four bags?

18 What can they see from the top of the volcano?

Chapter 7

Before you read

19 Check the words *paradise* and *altar* in your dictionary.

    a What is your idea of paradise?

    b Where can you find an altar?

20 What do you think will happen now to Arnold and Camilla? Do you think the islanders will help them?

21 Look at the picture on page 38. Do you think Arnold and Camilla's situation has improved? Why or why not?

After you read

22 Who asks these questions? Who are they speaking to?

    a 'Why are they here at all?'

    b 'Why did you come to Tanakuatua?'

    c 'What was this trick?'

    d 'So it was you who damaged the radio?'

23 What does Naeta say the spiders are doing?

24 What do Arnold and Camilla do to protect themselves against the spiders?

25 What do they find at the settlement?

Chapters 8–9

Before you read

26 Arnold and Camilla must now try to get off the island. How can they do this?

27 If you were in their situation what would you do first?

28 Look up the word *erupt* in your dictionary and write a sentence to show that you understand the meaning.

After you read

29 Answer these questions:

   a Why don't they hear the aeroplane?

   b What do the army officers think about Camilla and Arnold?

   c How does Lord Foxfield react to Camilla and Arnold's story of what happened on the island?

   d What happens to Lord Foxfield in the end?

   e What eventually happens to Tanakuatua?

   f Where is the last Little Sister found?

Writing

30 Lord Foxfield and Walter Tirrie wanted to start a new and better society on Tanakuatua. Without the spiders, do you think their project had any chance of succeeding? Explain why you would or would not want to join such a project and group of people.

31 Write about *Web*. Say why you think people should (or perhaps should not) read this book. Do you think the book has a useful message in it?

32 'John Wyndham is more interested in ideas than in people. His characters do not seem real, and so we do not care what happens to them.' Do you agree? Give reasons for your answer.

33 This book was written in the late 1960s. How do you think the story would be different if it were written today?

34 Do you feel sympathetic with the people of Tanakuatua? Why or why not? What would you do if a foreign government had bought your country and wanted you to leave it?

35 John Wyndham chose to write this story in the first person. What would be the advantages or disadvantages of writing it in the third person?